An Analysis of the Effect of the Economic Success of the BRIC Nations on the

Quad Nations and Union between Two Time Periods: 1991-2003 and 2004-2014.

Alan Bayham BA, MS

CHS, ASU, and UofP

Phoenix, Arizona USA

Abstract

This study is an analysis of the GDP, GNI, export, and import performance of the BRIC nations and the Quad nations and union between the 1991 to 2002 time period and the 2003 to 2014 time period. The hypothesis that the economic performance of the BRIC nations has negatively impacted the economic growth of the Quad nations and union between the 1991 to 2002 time period and the 2003 to 2014 time period was not found to be conclusively true because the Quad nations and union did well on all performance measures in the two time periods analyzed with the exception of the annual GDP mean performance. The BRIC nations, however, did outperform the Quad nations and union all economic measurements in this study as a group, which shows that, despite their higher annual GDP mean performance and the annual GNI mean performance, they have increased their exports and imports at a higher percentage than the Quad nations and union over the two periods measured.

Keywords: BRIC, Quad, developed, emerging, economic, performance

Information

Gross Domestic Product

The gross domestic product of a nation is used by economists as one of the primary economic indicators to measure the strength and health of countries economies (Investopedia, 2016). The GDP represents the total monetary value of all goods and services produced by a nation over a period of time, and it should be thought of as a representation of the size of a country's economy. Economists arrive at the figure of a country's GDP in one of two ways: by adding up the annual income of a nation or by adding up the money spent within a nation. The income approach is calculated by adding up employees' salaries, gross profits of companies within a nation, and taxes minus subsidies. The expenditure method, which is considered to be more common, is calculated by adding a nation's total consumption, investments, government spending, and net exports. A country's GDP figures, which show a nation's economic production and growth, impacts everyone within an economy because it reflects a country's economic health. Significant changes in a nation's GDP has a large impact on its unemployment rate, wage increases, and stock markets. Thus, poor GDP figures result in weakened economic growth for a nation, which results in fewer jobs, fewer profits, and lower stock prices. Negative GDP growth is what investors use to determine the strength of a nation's economy and whether or not it has entered an economic recession.

Gross National Income

Gross national income is the sum of a nation's GDP added to the net income received from other nations (Investopedia, 2016). GNI includes the sum of value added by producers of a nation, plus any taxes on products that are not included in the output, in addition to income received from abroad like employees' salaries or income gained from property holdings. GNI essentially measures a nation's domestic and overseas income. For most nations throughout the world, there is little difference between their GDP and GNI. For developed nations, like the US, their GNI is typically 1.5% higher than their GDP because of national organizations' investments in other countries. For some smaller economies throughout the world, like Ireland, there is a substantial difference between their GDP and GNI. Ireland attracts substantial foreign investment in comparison to the size of its economy, which has resulted in their GNI being about 20% lower than their GDP over the last couple of decades. Foreign investment in a nation is good because it contributes to economic growth, but most of the profits do not remain within the nation and return to the state in which the organization legally based. For smaller nations that attract foreign investment, the GNI can be a better indicator of economic performance and growth than the GDP.

GDP is a popular economic performance indicator for nations used by financial analysts around the world, but there are some limitations to it (Maverick, 2015). The measurement is considered to have deficiencies by economists because it fails to feature aspects of economic upturns and downturns to authentic changes in economies health or just cyclical changes. GDP analysis can also lead to excessive corrections by governments in which situations are created that lead to monetary policies that are tightened as a means to reduce inflation within economies. GDP fails to consider income earned outside of nations, so it can lead to threats of a recession that cause unnecessary reactions by central banks that result in easing restrictions on money supplies.

GNI calculations by the World Bank using the Atlas method is the sum of income added by all domestic producers, product taxes that do not include subsidies, and the total of compensation received from overseas employment or property holdings (The World Bank Group, 2016). The data offered by the WB is reported in US dollars, and official exchange rates are used to allow comparisons regarding GNI performance across national economies throughout the world. Alternative rates are used when official exchange rates diverge by large margins than the rates applied to international transactions.

Exports and Imports

Exports are a result of international trade and partnerships in which goods produced in one nation are shipped to another nation to sell or trade (Investopedia, 2016). Exporting is economically important because it adds to a nation's gross output, and, in instances in which they are used for trade, exports can be exchanged for products or services. History shows that exports are one of the oldest forms of economic transfer between nations and regions throughout the world, and exports have historically occurred at higher rates for nations that have fewer restrictions on trade and support free trade relationships. In advanced economies, the largest organizations derive a substantial amount of their annual revenues from exporting goods and services to other nations. Free trade among nations allows organizations to export goods with fewer tariffs and subsidies, and it results in greater economic growth for nations from selling more goods and services.

Imports are goods or services brought from one nation to another (Investopedia, 2016). Both exports and imports are considered to be the foundation of free trade among nations, and they can also be a source of economic debate within a country because the larger amount of imports entering a country in comparison to the amount and value of exports can lead to a trade deficit. Nations typically import goods and services that cannot be domestically produced as efficiently and at the cost of other nations, and this also includes the importation goods like raw materials and commodities that are not available domestically. Free trade agreements and customs duties guide the goods and materials that countries import, and this has dramatically shifted over the last two decades with increased trade agreements between nations. A good example would be the United States, which has increased its imports nearly 475% from $473 billion in 1989 to over $2.24 trillion in 2015.

In developed nations, free trade agreements and increasing reliance on imports from other nations because of cost savings have resulted in a decline in manufacturing centers and employment opportunities (Investopedia, 2016). Free trade allows nations to open up their markets to goods and materials from regions that can produce products for cheaper, and it reduces the reliance on domestically made goods. A good example would be the US economy, which has had a trade deficit since 1975. There are positive and negative results from the import goods from cheaper labor zones, but it results in the reliance on foreign-produced products. Products that are made more cheaply and imported by developed nations can enhance the quality of life in conjunction with assisting the prevention of inflation. The negative impact of importing goods from cheaper labor zones is that developed economies, which are democratic, indirectly support communistic countries, dictatorships, religious caste systems, and corrupt representative democracies.

Balance of Trade

A balance of trade is the difference between a nation's exports and imports, and it makes up the largest element of a nation's balance of international payments (Investopedia, 2016). Items that are debited on nation's balance of international payments include imports, aid, and domestic spending and trade to other countries, and items that are credited to a nation's balance of international payments are exports, foreign investments, and foreign spending in domestic economies. A nation has a trade deficit if it imports more than it exports, and a nation has a trade surplus if it exports more than it imports.

A nation's balance of trade is an often misinterpreted indicator of a national economy, and it is often believed by the public that trade deficits are a poor indication of a nation's economic performance (Investopedia, 2016). This, however, is not always true and is completely dependent on economic cycles within a nation. Typically, in recessions, nations like to export more than they import to increase employment rates and demand for goods. When a national economy is doing well, nations like to import more goods to increase price competition and decrease inflation, so trade deficits can be considered a bad thing during a recession and a good thing during a period of expansion.

Using a nation's trade balance as an economic indicator depends on the individual country because the largest impact regarding the balance of trade is seen within nations with limited foreign exchange reserves, which results in the release of data regarding trade that causes large fluctuations in national currencies (Investopedia, 2016). Collecting data regarding trade is easier for tangible exports and imports because it can be easily calculated from declarations and manifests, but the trade of intangible services has proven to be a bit more difficult and requires nations to compile statistics on the monetary flow of service industries. Thus, national statistics regarding imports and exports can be compiled from both trade statistics and balance of payments for tangible goods, but data regarding services can only be collected from a balance of payments.

The quality of balance of payment data for imports and exports to be used as an economic indicator depends on the nation, and the quality of reporting that is done by public and private organizations within it (Investopedia, 2016). Trade data is monitored closely by national economists and investors because they can act as a good indicator of an economy's health in a nation that adequately reports data for both imports and exports of both goods and services. Current account deficits, which the largest component of is trade data, is monitored for signs by government economists and investors as a precursor of the unmanageability of currencies, which can lead to the devaluation of national currencies. Temporary trade deficits in smaller nations can be seen as beneficial because it means that their economies are showing growth, and, in developed nations, it means that trade alliances are supporting free trade throughout the world and that national economic growth is being sustained. The bottom line is that the balance of trade within a nation is an important economic indicator of a nation's health, and, in general, national economists and investors are more concerned with trade deficits in comparison to trade surplus for smaller nations and developing economies because they can lead to a devaluation of a national currency.

BRIC Nations

The BRIC nations refer to the four largest rapidly emerging economies in the world: Brazil, Russia, India, and China (Koumparoulis, 2014). The term was conceived in 2001 as the BRIC economies began to grow rapidly and challenge the economic supremacy of developed nations. The BRIC nations have evolved differently over the last 15 years, and their economies have grown and contracted at different rates. In the first decade of the twenty-first century, the world saw an astonishing economic performance from the BRIC nations in comparison to developed nations and union like the United States, the European Union, Japan, and Canada. Since the termed was created and more than a decade has passed, the world has seen the BRIC economies continue to grow but at a slower rate in 2016 than was seen in the early part of the twenty-first century. There are a large number of nations that are now competing with the BRIC nations, which has resulted in a shift in growth from the BRIC economies to other emerging economies. They are essentially prospering for the same reasons that the BRIC nations have done well.

Quad Nations and Union

Over the last thirty years of international trade, there has been a major focus on the Quad, which is comprised of the United States, the European Union, Japan, and

Canada, because of the size of the economies and the benefits of developing economies in establish trade relations with these nations and union (Daly & Kuwahara, 1998). Although the Quad has remained a large economic force as world trade has expanded, there has been a large shift in investment from these nations by multinational organizations and investors to emerging economies throughout the world. This has empowered emerging economies and resulted in their new economic power being used to establish new trading partners. Despite the Quad still playing a leading role in global trade, the world has seen a shift in power to the emerging markets and dependence developed in Quad nations and union on goods from emerging market economies.

Purpose, Rationale, and Hypothesis

The purpose of this study was to analyze the GDP, GNI, export, and import performance of the BRIC nations and the Quad nations and union between the 1991 to 2002 time period and the 2003 to 2014 time period. The rationale behind the study was to analyze the BRIC nations' economic development and its impact on the Quad nations and union. The analysis used multiple measurements and data sets to analyze the growth and impact of the BRIC nations' economic growth on the Quad nations and union over the two time periods measured in relation to their GDP, GNI, export, and import performance. The hypothesis was that the economic performance of the BRIC nations has negatively impacted the economic growth of the Quad nations and union between the 1991 to 2002 time period and the 2003 to 2014 time period.

Methods

There were thirty-two measurements conducted in the analysis of the BRIC nations and the Quad nations and union between the 1991 to 2002 time period and the 2003 to 2014 time period. The first and second measurements collected and averaged the annual GDP mean performance of the BRIC nations for the 1991 to 2002 time period and the 2003 to 2014 time period. The third and fourth measurements calculated the percentage of change and the GDP shift of the BRIC nations between the 1991 to 2002 time period and the 2003 to 2014 time period. The fifth and sixth measurements collected and averaged the annual GDP mean performance of the Quad nations and union for the 1991 to 2002 time period and the 2003 to 2014 time period. The seventh and eighth measurements calculated the percentage of change and the GDP shift of the Quad nations and union between the 1991 to 2002 time period and the 2003 to 2014 time period. The ninth and tenth measurements collected and averaged the annual GNI mean performance of the BRIC nations for the 1991 to 2002 time period and the 2003 to 2014 time period. The eleventh and twelfth measurements calculated the percentage of change for the annual GNI mean performance and the annual GNI mean performance shift of the BRIC nations for the 1991 to 2002 time period and the 2003 to 2014 time period. The thirteenth and fourteenth measurements collected and averaged the annual GNI mean performance of the Quad nations and union for the 1991 to 2002 time period and the 2003 to 2014 time period. The fifteenth and sixteenth measurements calculated the percentage of change for the annual GNI mean performance and the annual GNI mean performance shift of the Quad nations and union for the 1991 to 2002 time period for the 1991 to 2002 time period and the 2003 to 2014 time period. The seventeenth and eighteenth measurements collected and averaged the annual export percentage of the GDP of the BRIC nations for the 1991 to 2002 time period and the 2003 to 2014 time period. The nineteenth and twentieth measurements calculated the percentage of change for the annual export percentage of the GDP and the annual export percentage of the GDP shift of the BRIC nations for the 1991 to 2002 time period and the 2003 to 2014 time period. The twenty-first and twenty-second measurements collected and averaged the annual export percentage of the GDP of the Quad nations and union for the 1991 to 2002 time period and the 2003 to 2014 time period. The twenty-third and twenty-fourth measurements calculated the percentage of change for the annual export percentage of the GDP and the annual export percentage of the GDP shift of the Quad nations and union for the 1991 to 2002 time period and the 2003 to 2014 time period. The twenty-fifth and twenty-sixth measurements collected and averaged the annual import percentage of the GDP of the BRIC nations for the 1991 to 2002 time period and the 2003 to 2014 time period. The twenty-seventh and twenty-eighth measurements calculated the percentage of change for the annual import percentage of the GDP and the annual import percentage of the GDP shift of the BRIC nations for the 1991 to 2002 time period and the 2003 to 2014 time period. The twenty-ninth and thirtieth measurements collected and averaged the annual import percentage of the GDP of the Quad nations and union for the 1991 to 2002 time period and the 2003 to 2014 time period. The thirty-first and thirty-second measurements calculated the percentage of change for the annual import percentage of the GDP and the annual import percentage of the GDP shift of the Quad nations and union for the 1991 to 2002 time period and the 2003 to 2014 time period.

Results

The first measurement collected and averaged the annual GDP mean performance of the BRIC nations for the 1991 to 2002 time period.

Country Name	Average 1991-2002
China	10.16630584
Brazil	2.557917233
India	5.385155567
Russian Federation	-2.185348652
	3.981007497

(The World Bank Group, 2016)

The second measurement collected and averaged the annual GDP mean performance of the BRIC nations for the 2003 to 2014 time period.

Country Name	Average 2003-2014
China	10.0005755
Brazil	3.46472332
India	7.722451446
Russian Federation	4.093191968
	6.320235559

(The World Bank Group, 2016)

The third measurement calculated the percentage of change from the 1991 and 2002 time period to the 2002 and 2014 for the annual GDP mean performance of the BRIC nations.

Country Name	Average 1991-2002	Average 2003-2014	% of Change
China	10.16630584	10.0005755	-0.016301923
Brazil	2.557917233	3.46472332	0.35450955
India	5.385155567	7.722451446	0.434025693
Russian Federation	-2.185348652	4.093191968	-2.873015532
	3.981007497	**6.320235559**	**0.587597**

(The World Bank Group, 2016)

The fourth measurement calculated the GDP shift from the 1991 and 2002 time period to the 2002 and 2014 for the annual GDP mean performance of the BRIC nations.

Country Name	Average 1991-2002	Average 2003-2014	GDP Shift
China	10.16630584	10.0005755	-0.16573034
Brazil	2.557917233	3.46472332	0.906806087
India	5.385155567	7.722451446	2.337295879
Russian Federation	-2.185348652	4.093191968	6.27854062
3.981007497	**6.320235559**	**2.339228062**

(The World Bank Group, 2016)

The fifth measurement collected and averaged the annual GDP mean performance of the Quad nations and union for the 1991 to 2002 time period.

Country Name	Average 1991-2002
United States	3.104674318
European Union	2.226803756
Canada	2.776313803
Japan	1.002171546
	2.277490856

(The World Bank Group, 2016)

The sixth measurement collected and averaged the annual GDP mean performance of the Quad nations and union for the 2003 to 2014 time period.

Country Name	Average 2003-2014
United States	1.864812
European Union	1.127138
Canada	2.001776
Japan	0.843909
	1.459409

(The World Bank Group, 2016)

The seventh measurement calculated the percentage of change from the 1991 and 2002 time period to the 2002 and 2014 for the annual GDP mean performance of the Quad nations and union.

Country Name	Average 1991-2002	Average 2003-2014	% of Change
United States	3.104674318	1.864812306	-0.399353325
European Union	2.226803756	1.127137791	-0.493831557
Canada	2.776313803	2.001776483	-0.278980467
Japan	1.002171546	0.843909161	-0.157919456
2.277490856	**1.459408935**	**-0.359203164**

(The World Bank Group, 2016)

The eighth measurement calculated the GDP shift from the 1991 and 2002 time period to the 2002 and 2014 for the annual GDP mean performance of the Quad nations and union.

Country Name	Average 1991-2002	Average 2003-2014	GDP Shift
United States	3.104674318	1.864812306	-1.239862012
European Union	2.226803756	1.127137791	-1.099665965
Canada	2.776313803	2.001776483	-0.77453732
Japan	1.002171546	0.843909161	-0.158262385
2.277490856	**1.459408935**	**-0.818081921**

(The World Bank Group, 2016)

The ninth measurement collected and averaged the annual GNI mean performance of the BRIC nations for the 1991 to 2002 time period.

Country Name	Average Mean 1991-2002
China	850032917015.05
Brazil	623339891452.71
India	401255155235.19

Russian Federation	362830143059.00
	559364526690.49

(The World Bank Group, 2016)

The tenth measurement collected and averaged the annual GNI mean performance of the BRIC nations for the 2003 to 2014 time period.

Country Name	Average Mean 2002-2014
China	5031688989733.76
Brazil	1533847923309.66
India	1331579367381.23
Russian Federation	1234004037954.45
	2282780079594.78

(The World Bank Group, 2016)

The eleventh measurement calculated the percentage of change from the 1991 and 2002 time period to the 2002 and 2014 for the annual GNI mean performance of the BRIC nations.

Country Name	Average Mean 1991-2002	Average Mean 2002-2014	% of Change
China	850032917015.05	5031688989733.76	4.919404871
Brazil	623339891452.71	1533847923309.66	1.460692704
India	401255155235.19	1331579367381.23	2.318535226
Russian Federation	362830143059.00	1234004037954.45	2.401051598
	559364526690.49	**2282780079594.78**	**3.081024038**

(The World Bank Group, 2016)

The twelfth measurement calculated the GNI shift from the 1991 and 2002 time period to the 2002 and 2014 for the annual GNI mean performance of the BRIC nations.

Country Name	Average Mean 1991-2002	Average Mean 2002-2014	GNI Shift
China	850032917015.05	5031688989733.76	4181656072718.71

Brazil	623339891452.71	1533847923309.66	910508031856.95
India	401255155235.19	1331579367381.23	930324212146.04
Russian Federation	362830143059.00	1234004037954.45	871173894895.45
	559364526690.49	**2282780079594.78**	**1723415552904.29**

The thirteenth measurement collected and averaged the annual GNI mean performance of the Quad nations and union for the 1991 to 2002 time period.

Country Name	Average Mean 1991-2002
European Union	9030676690583.91
Japan	4418398635778.81
United States	8434616257700.39
Canada	638243692519.06
	5630483819145.54

The fourteenth measurement collected and averaged the annual GNI mean performance of the Quad nations and union for the 2003 to 2014 time period.

Country Name	Average Mean 1991-2002
European Union	9030676690583.91
Japan	4418398635778.81
United States	8434616257700.39
Canada	638243692519.06
	5630483819145.54

The fifteenth measurement calculated the percentage of change from the 1991 and 2002 time period to the 2002 and 2014 for the annual GNI mean performance of the Quad nations and union.

Country Name	Average Mean 1991-2002	Average Mean 2002-2014	% of Change

European Union	9030676690583.91	16308435497750.40	0.805892964
Japan	4418398635778.81	5163423213777.75	0.168618687
United States	8434616257700.39	14899826271362.30	0.766509088
Canada	638243692519.06	1410765630718.97	1.21038711
	5630483819145.54	**9445612653402.37**	**0.677584548**

(The World Bank Group, 2016)

The sixteenth measurement calculated the GNI shift from the 1991 and 2002 time period to the 2002 and 2014 for the annual GNI mean performance of the Quad nations and union.

Country Name	Average Mean 1991-2002	Average Mean 2002-2014	GNI Shift
European Union	9030676690583.91	16308435497750.40	7277758807166.49
Japan	4418398635778.81	5163423213777.75	745024577998.94
United States	8434616257700.39	14899826271362.30	6465210013661.91
Canada	638243692519.06	1410765630718.97	772521938199.91
	5630483819145.54	**9445612653402.37**	**3815128834256.83**

(The World Bank Group, 2016)

The seventeenth measurement collected and averaged the annual export percentage of the GDP of the BRIC nations for the 1991 to 2002 time period.

Country Name	Average Mean 1991-2002
Brazil	9.576900228
China	19.29343358
India	11.58503097
Russian Federation	34.47580282
	18.7327919

(The World Bank Group, 2016)

The eighteenth measurement collected and averaged the annual export percentage of the GDP of the BRIC nations for the 2003 to 2014 time period.

Country Name	Average Mean 2003-2014
Brazil	12.98699365
China	28.21888922
India	21.30787451
Russian Federation	31.30657259
	23.45508249

(The World Bank Group, 2016)

The nineteenth measurement calculated the percentage of change from the 1991 and 2002 time period to the 2002 and 2014 for the annual export percentage of the GDP of the BRIC nations.

Country Name	Average Mean 1991-2002	Average Mean 2003-2014	% of Change
Brazil	9.576900228	12.98699365	0.356074861
China	19.29343358	28.21888922	0.462616237
India	11.58503097	21.30787451	0.839259175
Russian Federation	34.47580282	31.30657259	-0.09192622
	18.7327919	**23.45508249**	**0.252086855**

(The World Bank Group, 2016)

The twentieth measurement calculated the annual export percentage of the GDP shift from the 1991 and 2002 time period to the 2002 and 2014 for the annual export percentage of the GDP of the BRIC nations.

Country Name	Average Mean 1991-2002	Average Mean 2003-2014	Export Shift
Brazil	9.576900228	12.98699365	3.410093422
China	19.29343358	28.21888922	8.92545564
India	11.58503097	21.30787451	9.72284354
Russian Federation	34.47580282	31.30657259	-3.16923023
	18.7327919	**23.45508249**	**4.72229059**

(The World Bank Group, 2016)

The twenty-first measurement collected and averaged the annual export percentage of the GDP of the Quad nations and union for the 1991 to 2002 time period.

Country Name	Average Mean 1991-2002
European Union	29.57045121
United States	10.10935357
Japan	10.05978975
Canada	36.13014118
	21.46743393

(The World Bank Group, 2016)

The twenty-second measurement collected and averaged the annual export percentage of the GDP of the BRIC nations for the 2003 to 2014 time period.

Country Name	Average Mean 2003-2014
European Union	37.77050425
United States	11.73600142
Japan	15.21491798
Canada	32.98045842
	24.42547052

(The World Bank Group, 2016)

The twenty-third measurement calculated the percentage of change from the 1991 and 2002 time period to the 2002 and 2014 for the annual export percentage of the GDP of the Quad nations and union.

Country Name	Average Mean 1991-2002	Average Mean 2003-2014	% of Change
European Union	29.57045121	37.77050425	0.277305645
United States	10.10935357	11.73600142	0.160905229
Japan	10.05978975	15.21491798	0.512448904
Canada	36.13014118	32.98045842	-0.087176044
	21.46743393	**24.42547052**	**0.137791811**

(The World Bank Group, 2016)

The twenty-fourth measurement calculated the annual export percentage of the GDP shift from the 1991 and 2002 time period to the 2002 and 2014 for the annual export percentage of the GDP of the Quad nations and union.

Country Name	Average Mean 1991-2002	Average Mean 2003-2014	Export Shift
European Union	29.57045121	37.77050425	8.20005304
United States	10.10935357	11.73600142	1.62664785
Japan	10.05978975	15.21491798	5.15512823
Canada	36.13014118	32.98045842	-3.14968276
	21.46743393	**24.42547052**	**2.95803659**

(The World Bank Group, 2016)

The twenty-fifth measurement collected and averaged the annual import percentage of the GDP of the BRIC nations for the 1991 to 2002 time period.

Country Name	Average Mean 1991-2002
Brazil	10.33752613
China	17.04222433
India	11.64698785
Russian Federation	25.71953809
	16.1865691

The twenty-sixth measurement collected and averaged the annual import percentage of the GDP of the BRIC nations for the 2003 to 2014 time period.

Country Name	Average Mean 2003-2014
Brazil	12.62885764
China	24.34048714
India	25.10962682
Russian Federation	21.94914452
	21.00702903

(The World Bank Group, 2016)

The twenty-seventh measurement calculated the percentage of change from the 1991 and 2002 time period to the 2002 and 2014 for the annual import percentage of the GDP of the BRIC nations.

Country Name	Average Mean 1991-2002	Average Mean 2003-2014	% of Change
Brazil	10.33752613	12.62885764	0.221651823
China	17.04222433	24.34048714	0.428245907
India	11.64698785	25.10962682	1.155890188
Russian Federation	25.71953809	21.94914452	-0.146596473
	16.1865691	**21.00702903**	**0.297806156**

(The World Bank Group, 2016)

The twenty-eighth measurement calculated the annual import percentage of the GDP shift from the 1991 and 2002 time period to the 2002 and 2014 for the annual import percentage of the GDP of the BRIC nations.

Country Name	Average Mean 1991-2002	Average Mean 2003-2014	Import Shift
Brazil	10.33752613	12.62885764	2.29133151
China	17.04222433	24.34048714	7.29826281
India	11.64698785	25.10962682	13.46263897
Russian Federation	25.71953809	21.94914452	-3.77039357
	16.1865691	**21.00702903**	**4.82045993**

(The World Bank Group, 2016)

The twenty-ninth measurement collected and averaged the annual import percentage of the GDP of the Quad nations and union for the 1991 to 2002 time period.

Country Name	Average Mean 1991-2002
European Union	28.66511679
United States	11.96014266
Japan	8.588349682
Canada	33.59213709
	20.70143655

The thirtieth measurement collected and averaged the annual import percentage of the GDP of the Quad nations and union for the 2003 to 2014 time period.

Country Name	Average Mean 2003-2014
European Union	36.60583297
United States	15.88996986
Japan	15.14034452
Canada	32.16677523
	24.95073064

(The World Bank Group, 2016)

The thirty-first measurement calculated the percentage of change from the 1991 and 2002 time period to the 2002 and 2014 for the annual import percentage of the GDP of the Quad nations and union.

Country Name	Average Mean 1991-2002	Average Mean 2003-2014	% of Change
European Union	28.66511679	36.60583297	0.277016704
United States	11.96014266	15.88996986	0.32857695
Japan	8.588349682	15.14034452	0.762893347
Canada	33.59213709	32.16677523	-0.042431414
	20.70143655	**24.95073064**	**0.205265663**

(The World Bank Group, 2016)

The thirty-second measurement calculated the annual import percentage of the GDP shift from the 1991 and 2002 time period to the 2002 and 2014 for the annual import percentage of the GDP of the Quad nations and union.

Country Name	Average Mean 1991-2002	Average Mean 2003-2014	Import Shift
European Union	28.66511679	36.60583297	7.94071618
United States	11.96014266	15.88996986	3.9298272
Japan	8.588349682	15.14034452	6.551994838
Canada	33.59213709	32.16677523	-1.42536186
	20.70143655	**24.95073064**	**4.24929409**

Discussion

The first, second, third, and fourth measurements analyzed the annual GDP mean performance of the BRIC nations and compared the annual GDP mean performance between the 1991 to 2002 time period and 2003 to 2014 time period.

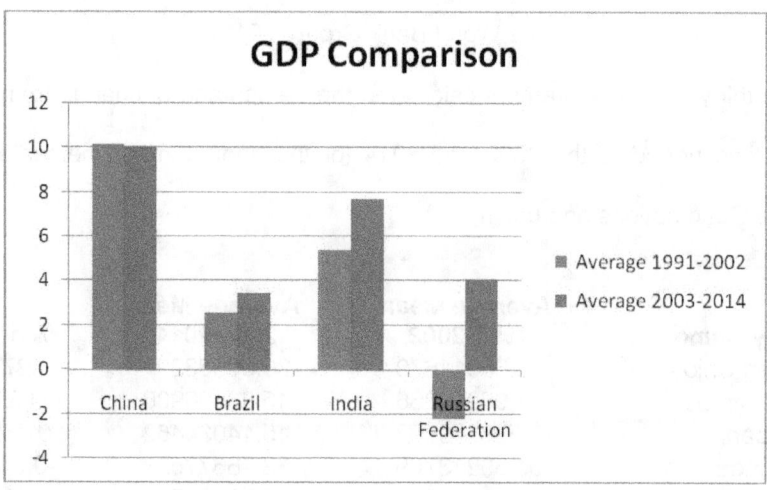

As can be seen in the above chart, the annual GDP mean performance between the two time periods shows a slight decrease in performance for China and substantial annual GDP mean performance for the other nations, especially the Russian Federation. The average performance annual GDP mean performance of the BRIC nations was 3.98 for the 1991 to 2002 time period and 6.32 for the 2003 to 2014 time period, so there was a positive annual GDP mean performance shift between the two time periods measured for the BRIC nations of 2.34. Brazil's economy grew 35% between the 1991 to 2002 time and 2003 to 2014, India's economy grew 43% between the 1991 to 2002 time and 2003 to 2014, and Russia's economy grew the most between the 1991 to 2002 time and 2003 to 2014 at 287%. China's economy contracted by 2% when comparing the 1991 to 2002 time period and 2003 to 2014 time period, but it had the largest annual GDP mean performance for all the BRIC nations for the two time periods at 10.17 for the 1991 to 2002 time period and 10 for the 2003 to 2014 time period. For the BRIC nations economies to improve and to encourage economic growth, new strategies and policies were needed to stimulate growth within their nations, and, from the data analyzed, it can be concluded that they were implemented and successful (Srinivasan, 2014). Policies and strategies drove growth in the Russian Federation, India, and China, but, in Brazil, economic growth was driven more by policies than strategy. These offered both incentives and subsidies to organizations exporting goods from the nation, and the government set up specialized Export Processing Zones that proved to be successful for merchants within the nation. For the Russian Federation, India, and China, economic growth continually intensified as their economies became larger and more powerful, and they continue to work to the present day to make their exports competitive on the global market, to improve productivity levels of their export sectors, and to diversify their export of commodities. This includes further infrastructure development and reduction of trade barriers within these nations in conjunction with increased incentives and subsidies, specifically to exporters in Brazil in their EPZs. For further growth within the BRIC nations, legislation should continue to be enacted and policy measures should be adopted that continue to enlarge and diversify their economic basis to continue to promote growth, improve their national and domestic economies, and improve the economic stability in combination with improving the lives and educational level of citizens of their nations.

The fifth, sixth, seventh, and eighth measurements analyzed the annual GDP mean performance of the Quad nations and union when comparing the annual GDP mean performance between the 1991 to 2002 time period and 2003 to 2014 time period.

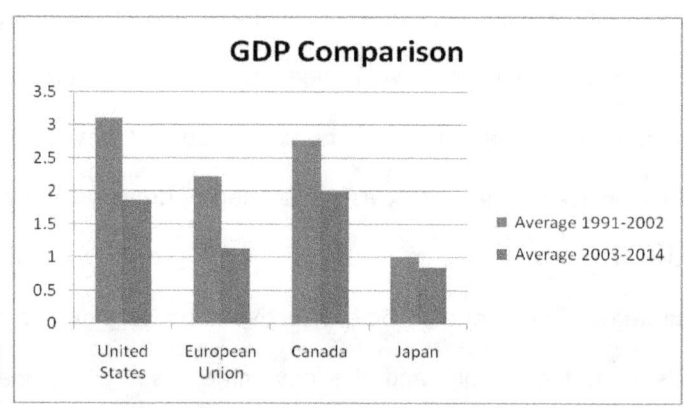

As can be seen in the above chart, the annual GDP mean performance between the two time periods shows economic contractions between the two time periods for all of the Quad nations and union in relation to their annual GDP mean performance, especially for the US and the EU. The average annual GDP mean for the Quad nations and union was 2.28 for the 1991 to 2002 time period and 1.46, which shows a negative annual GDP mean performance shift of .82. The US's economy contracted by 40% in comparison between the 1991 to 2002 time and 2003 to 2014 in relation to its annual GDP mean performance, the EU's economy contracted by 49% in comparison between the 1991 to 2002 time and 2003 to 2014 in relation to its annual GDP mean performance, Canada's economy contracted by 40% in comparison between the 1991 to 2002 time and 2003 to 2014 in relation to its annual GDP mean performance, and Japan's economy contracted by 16% in comparison between the 1991 to 2002 time and

2003 to 2014 in relation to its annual GDP mean performance. The economic problems seen in the Quad nations and union between the 2003 to 2014 period can be attributed to a lack of structural reforms, especially in the EU, and slowing economic growth in comparison to the size of national debt these nations have (Alexeev, 2014). The rate of economic growth in the Quad nations and union threatens to weaken their economies, increase budget deficits, and enlarge healthcare expenses. The unusually budget deficit, especially in the US, is a result of the economic situation in which organizations nationwide have offshored manufacturing and development for higher profits, which has resulted in high unemployment and low federal taxation within the nation. Another problem that exists is a decline in the level of innovation, specifically in Europe, outside of the communications and technology sector because Western nations have exhausted their ability to advance nations' educational levels, specifically that of children. As employment has shifted from Western nations to developing countries where copyright laws are virtually non-existent, Western nations have had less of an incentive to invest time and money in research and development, which leads to the innovating technologies being used throughout the world today. Emerging economies, like China, have achieved unprecedented economic growth for decades through the use of Western technologies and annual migration patterns of poor, uneducated citizens from rural areas seeking employment in larger cities. It is estimated by analysts that over time these innovative patterns will continue to weaken in conjunction with a weakening of BRIC nations economies as a result of changing population demographics and offshoring to even less developed nations. This slowdown will be dangerous for the BRIC nations, especially China, because they have spent large sums of money on resources and investment projects with very little potential for return, such as: high-speed railways, real estate development, and other projects in small Third World nations with unstable governments and social situations. Also, the BRIC nations' ecology has suffered tremendously as a result of poor infrastructure, government regulation, and corruption, which has depleted the quality of life for the masses despite their large and recent economic growth. Most alarming is the banking situation in the BRIC nations, which has shown them to be ineffective in controlling real estate prices, stock markets, currency fluctuation, and dealing with global economic changes.

The ninth, tenth, eleventh, and twelfth measurements analyzed the annual GNI mean performance of the BRIC nations compared the annual GNI mean performance between the 1991 to 2002 time period and 2003 to 2014 time period.

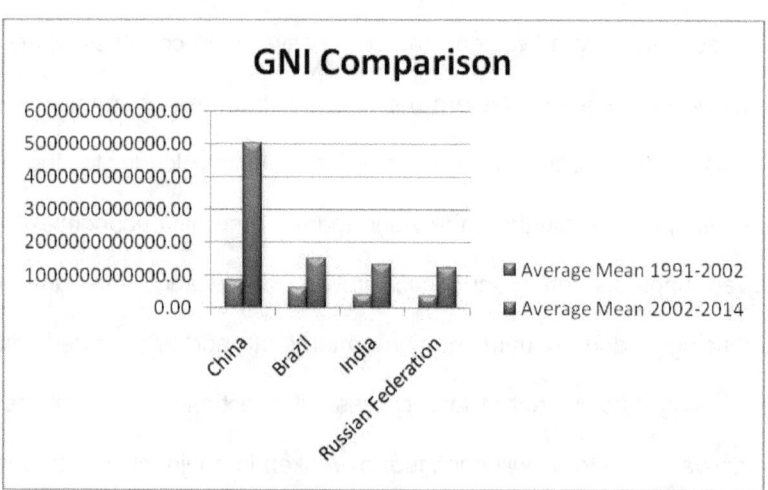

As can be seen in the above chart, the annual GNI mean performance between the two time periods shows a large increase in performance for all BRIC nations, especially China. The average annual GNI mean performance for the BRIC nations between the

1991 to 2002 time period was 559364526690.49, and the average annual GNI mean performance for the BRIC nations between the 2003 to 2014 time period was 2282780079594.78. Thus, there was a positive annual GNI performance shift of 1723415552904.29 for the BRIC nations between the two time periods measured. China's annual GNI mean performance increased by 492% when comparing the 1991 to 2002 time period and 2003 to 2014 time period, Brazil's annual GNI mean performance increased by 146% when comparing the 1991 to 2002 time period and 2003 to 2014 time period, India's annual GNI mean performance increased by 232% when comparing the 1991 to 2002 time period and 2003 to 2014 time period, and the Russian Federation's annual GNI mean performance increased by 240% when comparing the 1991 to 2002 time period and 2003 to 2014 time period. The growth of the middle class in relations to annual GDP mean performance and annual GNI performance between the 1991 to 2002 time period and 2003 to 2014 time period has been substantial and changed improved the living standards of millions of people within the BRIC nations (Kapas & Liang, 2009). The reality is that in the emerging markets even modest economic growth can greatly increase the number of individuals who are considered to be middle class within the BRIC nations because of the size of the middle class previous to the last couple of decades of substantial annual GDP mean performance and annual GNI performance was extremely small in comparison to their overall population size. Some analysts anticipate that the size of the middle class in the BRIC nations will make up over 40% of the population by 2030. This substantial growth of the middle class will translate into increased demand by the middle class within these nations and larger control of the world's GDP.

The thirteenth, fourteenth, fifteenth, and sixteenth measurements analyzed the annual GNI mean performance of the Quad nations and union between the 1991 to 2002 time period and 2003 to 2014 time period.

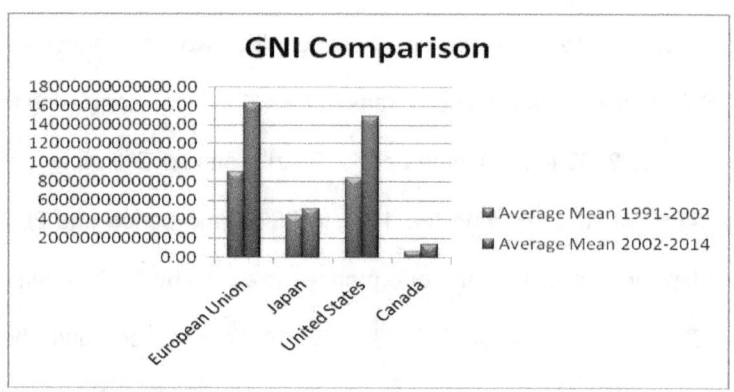

As can be seen in the above chart, the annual GNI mean performance between the two time periods shows a performance increase for all of the Quad nations and union, especially Canada. The average annual GNI mean performance for the Quad nations and union was 5630483819145.54 for the 1991 to 2002 time period and was 9445612653402.37 for the 2003 to 2014 time period. This shows an average annual GNI mean positive performance shift for the Quad nations of 3815128834256.83 between the two time periods measured. The United States' GNI increased by 77% when comparing between the 1991 to 2002 time period and 2003 to 2014 time period, the European Union's GNI increased by 81% when comparing between the 1991 to 2002 time period and 2003 to 2014 time period, Japan's GNI increased by 17% when comparing between the 1991 to 2002 time period and 2003 to 2014 time period, and the Canada's GNI increased by 121% when comparing between the 1991 to 2002 time period and 2003 to 2014 time period. This data shows that Canada, the European

Union, and the United States have had strong annual GNI performance between the two time periods measured, which shows that these nations and union are deriving substantial amounts of income from other nations in relation to employee salaries and money gained from properties owned. The growth of free trade has intensified competition for the Quad nations and union, but it has resulted in a group of affluent consumers in emerging markets like the BRIC nations (European Commission, 2016). Over the last 20 years, the BRIC nations' tariffs have fallen between from 30% to 70%, which is product and nation specific. This is a substantial decline, and it shows that these markets are slowly opening up to free trade with other nations, specifically the Quad nations and union. Some economic analysts anticipate that increased free trade with the emerging markets will increase jobs and promote economic growth. The International Monetary Fund is estimating that 90% of the future economic growth in the world will be outside of Europe and in the emerging markets.

The seventeenth, eighteenth, nineteenth, and twentieth measurements analyzed the percentage of change of the annual export percentage of the GDP of the BRIC nations between the 1991 to 2002 time period and 2003 to 2014 time period.

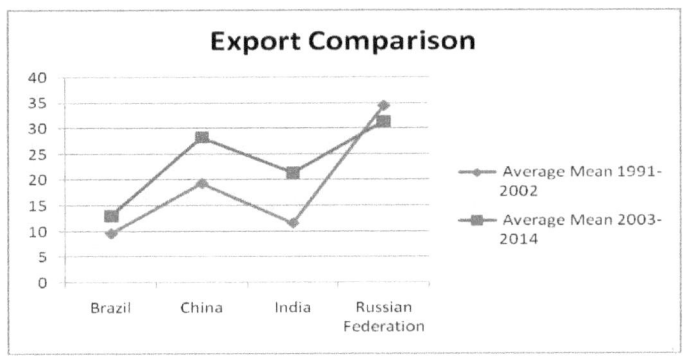

As can be seen in the above chart, the annual export percentage of the GDP of the BRIC nations between the 1991 to 2002 time period and 2003 to 2014 time period shows a large increase in performance for all BRIC nations, especially China and India. The average annual export percentage of the GDP of the BRIC nations between the 1991 to 2002 time period was 18.73, and the average annual export percentage of the GDP of the BRIC nations between the 2003 to 2014 time period was 23.46. Thus, there was a positive average annual export percentage shift of the GDP of the BRIC nations of 4.72 between the two time periods measured. China's annual export percentage of its GDP increased by 46% between the 1991 to 2002 time period and 2003 to 2014 time period, Brazil's annual export percentage of its GDP increased by 36% between the 1991 to 2002 time period and 2003 to 2014 time period, and India's annual export percentage of its GDP increased by 84% between the 1991 to 2002 time period and 2003 to 2014 time period. The Russian Federation's annual export percentage of its GDP decreased by 9% between the 1991 to 2002 time period and 2003 to 2014 time period, but the Russian Federation had the largest annual export percentage of its GDP of all the BRIC nations in both time periods at 34.48 for the 1991 to 2002 time period and 31.31 for the 2003 to 2014 time period. The main exports from Brazil are mineral products, vegetable products, foodstuffs, transportation goods, machines, metals, and chemical products (Macro Connections, 2016). The main exports from Russia are mineral products, metals, chemical products, precious metals, and machines. The main exports from India are mineral products, textiles, chemical products, machines, metals, transportation goods, vegetable products, precious metals, and plastics and rubber. The main exports from China are machines, textiles, metals, household products, chemical products, plastics and rubber, transportation goods, and instrumentation. The expansion of the BRIC nations' economies has increased global trade and improved the lives of people within these nations. It has also assisted in keeping inflation relatively low over the last couple of decades and improved the domestic markets of nations importing the BRIC nations' goods. It, however, has led to a decrease in employment in some sectors in developed nations, and the dependence it has created concerns some economists. Offshoring and outsourcing from multinational organizations has resulted in increased profits for the organizations and their investors, and it has increased international trade as a result moving portions of jobs or entire jobs to emerging markets, specifically the BRIC nations (Kumar, 2013). Since the mid-1980s, the number of employees for US multinational organizations has nearly doubled, and it has resulted in expanding the traded goods sector between developed nations and emerging economies, increased the output and export of emerging economies, and led to job reduction in specific sectors in America. Offshoring and outsourcing to developing economies also leads to large expansions in nontraded sectors within these nations, which results in increased employment rates, better paying jobs, and a higher standard of living for these nations. Offshoring and outsourcing in conjunction with lowered trade barriers has permitted emerging economies to make their goods and services competitive on the world market, especially to developed nations. Despite the loss of jobs resulting in specific sectors from offshoring and outsourcing to emerging economies, there has been a remarkable decline in inflation worldwide because of a decrease in prices on traded goods. Another result of offshoring and outsourcing, seen in developed countries, is a steady increase in the cost of nontraded goods, such as:

education, legal services, healthcare, and housing. This has worked as a natural tariff in developed economies to mitigate factor-price equalization or the equalization of wages, capital, and housing across these nations as a result of international trade.

The twenty-first, twenty-second, twenty-third, and twenty-fourth measurements analyzed the percentage of change of the annual export percentage of the GDP of the Quad nations between the 1991 to 2002 time period and 2003 to 2014 time period.

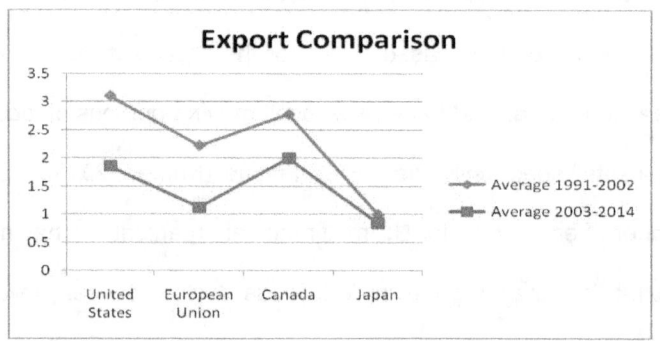

As can be seen in the above chart, the annual export percentage of the GDP of the Quad nations between the 1991 to 2002 time period and 2003 to 2014 time period shows a large decrease in performance for all Quad nations and union, especially the United States, the European Union, and Canada. The average annual export percentage of the GDP of the Quad nations and union was 21.46743393 for the 1991 to 2002 time period and was 24.42547052 for the 2003 to 2014 time period, which shows a negative annual export percentage shift of the GDP of the Quad nations and union at 2.95803659. The United States' annual export percentage of its GDP decreased by 40% between the 1991 to 2002 time period and 2003 to 2014 time period, the European Union's annual export percentage of its GDP decreased by 49% between the 1991 to 2002 time period and 2003 to 2014 time period, Canada's annual export percentage of its GDP increased by 28% between the 1991 to 2002 time period and 2003 to 2014 time period, and Japan's annual export percentage of its GDP increased by 16% between the 1991 to 2002 time period and 2003 to 2014 time period. The US's main exports are machines, transportation goods, chemical products, instruments, plastics and rubber, metals, vegetable products, foodstuffs, and precious metals (Macro Connections, 2016). The EU's main exports are machinery and transport equipment, manufactured goods, foodstuffs and tobacco, minerals, and raw materials (Eurostat, 2016). Japan's main exports are machines, transportation goods, metals, chemical products, instruments, plastics and rubber, and minerals (Macro Connections, 2016). Canada's main exports are mineral products, transportation goods, machines, metals, chemical products, vegetable products, plastics and rubber, paper goods, precious metals, wood products, animal products, and foodstuffs. Increased free trade over the last three decades in conjunction with offshoring, outsourcing, and foreign direct investment have led to trade imbalances between developed nations and emerging economies (Crino & Epifani, 2014). These trade imbalances have resulted in declining exports from developed economies and increased competitiveness because of price advantages resulting in labor cost savings, which has caused a loss of employment and rising skill premia in many sectors in developed nations. The market share of world merchandise has declined over the last three decades, and many emerging nations' economies have shifted from being competitive in exporting goods to being increasingly aggressive in the export of their services as well (Mandel, 2012). A good example would be the US in which 12% of the goods shipped globally originated in the nation throughout the 80s and 90s but has since declined to 3.5%. The shift of exports from emerging markets in world trade has been caused by a number of factors, but it does not show a great loss of productivity of export sectors of developed nations as a group. A decline in exports in developed nations is a result of global shifts in exports and a change in the size of economies from emerging market nations. This does not mean that developed nations are less competitive, but it does show a global shift in exports and the dynamics of GDPs. The decline in exports from developed nations has resulted from commodity prices, trade costs, and outsourcing, but it does not reflect a lack of competiveness.

The twenty-fifth, twenty-sixth, twenty-seventh, and twenty-eighth measurements analyzed the percentage of change of the annual import percentage of the GDP of the BRIC nations between the 1991 to 2002 time period and 2003 to 2014 time period.

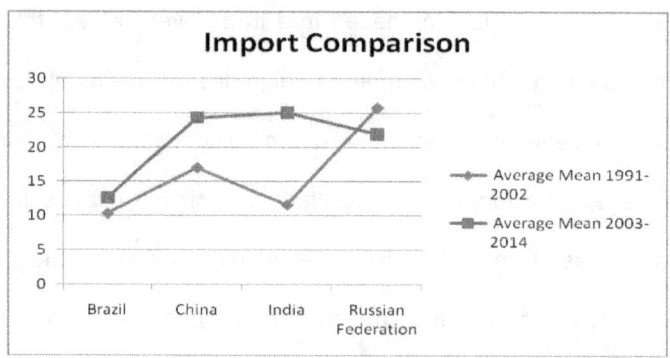

As can be seen in the above chart, the annual import percentage of the GDP of the BRIC nations between the 1991 to 2002 time period and 2003 to 2014 time period shows a large increase in performance for most BRIC nations, especially China and India. The average annual import percentage of the GDP of the BRIC nations between 1991 and 2002 was 16.1865691, and the average annual import percentage of the GDP of the BRIC nations between 2003 and 2014 was 21.00702903. This shows a positive average annual import percentage shift of the GDP of the BRIC nations of 4.82045993 between the two periods measured. As a group, the annual import percentage of the GDP of the BRIC nations between the 1991 to 2002 time period and 2003 to 2014 time period increased by 30%. China's annual import percentage of its GDP increased by 43% when comparing between the 1991 to 2002 time period and 2003 to 2014 time period, Brazil's annual import percentage of its GDP increased by 22% when comparing between the 1991 to 2002 time period and 2003 to 2014 time period, and India's annual export percentage of its GDP increased by 115% when comparing between the 1991 to 2002 time period and 2003 to 2014 time period. The Russian Federation's annual import percentage of its GDP decreased by 15% between the 1991 to 2002 time period and 2003 to 2014 time period, but the Russian Federation had the largest annual import percentage of its GDP of all the BRIC nations for the 1991 to 2002 time period at 25.72 and the third largest annual import percentage of its GDP of all the BRIC nations for the 2003 to 2014 time period at 21.95 behind India and China.

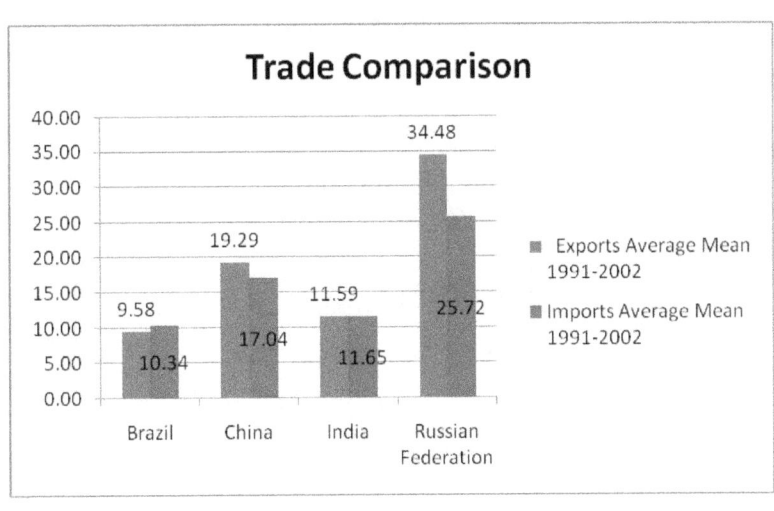

The data shows that two of the BRIC nations had trade surpluses in an analysis of their annual import and export percentages of the GDP for the 1991 to 2002 time period. Brazil showed a trade deficit of .76 for 1991 to 2002 time period, and India showed a trade deficit at .06 for India 1991 to 2002 time period. Russia showed the largest difference of annual import and export percentage of the GDP for the 1991 to 2002 time period with a trade surplus of 8.76. The main imports to these nations differ in relation to their economies, and their dependence on international trade for national domestic markets. Brazil's main imports are machines, minerals, chemical products, goods for transport, metals, and plastics and rubber (Macro Connections, 2016). Russia's main imports are mineral products, chemical products, metals, textiles, and plastics. India's main imports are mineral products, machines, precious metals, chemical products, metals, and plastics. China's main imports are mineral products, machines, goods for transportation, chemical products, plastics and rubber, instruments, and precious metals. These indirectly support other key export industries for these nations, so their imports have increased as a result of their expanding exports over the last couple of decades.

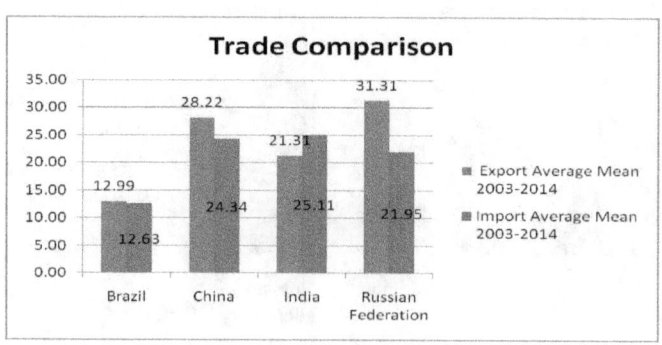

Most of the BRIC nations increased imports are a result of increased trade with developing markets throughout the world, and it is clear that as new emerging markets grow that the BRIC nations are capitalizing on trade relations with them (Castro, 2013). The one exception to this is the Russian Federation, which imported more goods from developed countries than other emerging markets. India was also the only BRIC nation to show a trade deficit between the 2003 to 2014 time period at 3.8. The level of exports versus imports to the BRIC nations has resulted in trade surpluses over the two time periods measured for most of the countries, which has clearly benefitted their economies. The exceptions to this out the BRIC nations would be Brazil and India from the 1991 to 2002 time period and India during the 2003 to 2014 time period. During these time periods, these BRIC nations imported more goods than they exported, but the general trend is an increase in both exports and imports for most of the BRIC nations, which has led to trade surpluses.

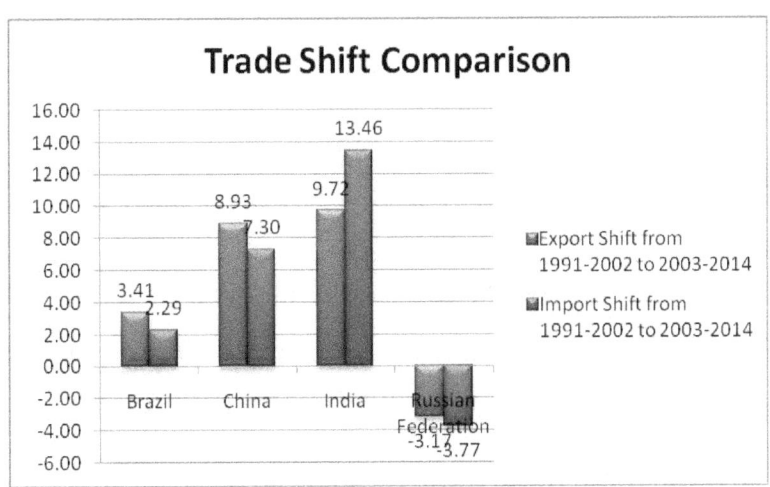

Both imports and exports of goods and services increased for all of the BRIC nations with the exception of the Russian Federation between the two time periods measured.

The Russian Federation led all BRIC nations with the largest annual export percentage of its GDP at 34.48 for the 1991 to 2002 time period and 31.31 for the 2003 to 2014 time period. The Russian Federation also led all BRIC nations with the largest annual import percentage of its GDP at 25.72 for the 1991 to 2002 time period, but it only had the third largest annual import percentage of its GDP at 31.95 for the 2003 to 214 time period behind India and China.

The twenty-ninth, thirtieth, thirty-first, and thirty-second measurements analyzed the percentage of change of the annual import percentage of the GDP of the Quad nations and union between the 1991 to 2002 time period and 2003 to 2014 time period.

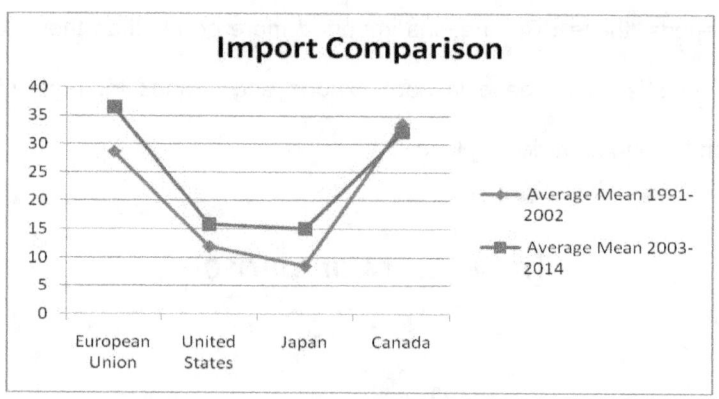

As can be seen in the above chart, the annual import percentage of the GDP of the Quad nations and union between the 1991 to 2002 time period and 2003 to 2014 time shows a moderate increase in performance for most Quad nations and with a 21% increase in imports for the group between the two time periods measured. The average annual import percentage of the GDP of the Quad nations and union between the 1991 and 2002 was 20.70143655, and the average annual import percentage of the GDP of the Quad nations and union between the 2003 and 2014 was 24.95073064. Thus, there was a positive average annual import percentage shift of the GDP at 4.25. Canada showed a negative annual import percentage shift of the GDP between the 1991 to 2002 time period and the 2003 to 2014 time period at 1.43. Canada, however, had the largest annual import percentage of its GDP of all of the Quad nations and union between the 1991 to 2002 period at 33.59, and it has the second largest annual import percentage of its GDP at 32.17 for the 2003 to 2014 time period. The EU showed the largest annual positive import percentage GDP shift between the two time periods measured at 7.94, and Japan showed the second largest positive annual import percentage of its GDP shift between the two time periods measured at 6.55. The EU's annual import percentage of its GDP increased by 28% between the 1991 to 2002 time period and 2003 to 2014 time period, the US's annual import percentage of its GDP increased by 33% between the 1991 to 2002 time period and 2003 to 2014 time period, and Japan's annual export percentage of its GDP increased by 76% between the 1991 to 2002 time period and 2003 to 2014 time period. Canada's annual import percentage of its GDP decreased by 5% between the 1991 to 2002 time period and 2003 to 2014 time period. International trade among nations throughout the world affects every person living in a developed nation (Williams & Donnelly, 2012). Free trade and the agreements that have put trading partnerships in place around the world have made products and services available from all over the world in developed nations, such as: clothing, gas, computers, cars, and much more. The three largest exporters in the world are China, Germany, and the US, but, despite the large amount of exports from these nations, the US is the only one with a trade deficit. China has had a trade surplus since 1995, and Germany has had a trade surplus since 1952 (Trading Economics,

2016). The US and most Western nations' exports are overshadowed by the demand for imports required by national consumers, and the US has had a retail trade deficit since 1976 (Williams & Donnelly, 2012). Trade balance consist of deficits or surpluses with individual trading partners, and most economists view overall balances as more important than bilateral trade deficits or surpluses because rising deficits are often offset by trade surpluses with other trading partners. Large and rapidly increasing trade deficits with specific trading partners, however, are an indication that underlying problem may exist for market access in relation to bilateral trade. These problems persist as a result of a lack of market access, a nation's competitiveness in industries, misaligned currencies, or macroeconomic adjustments.

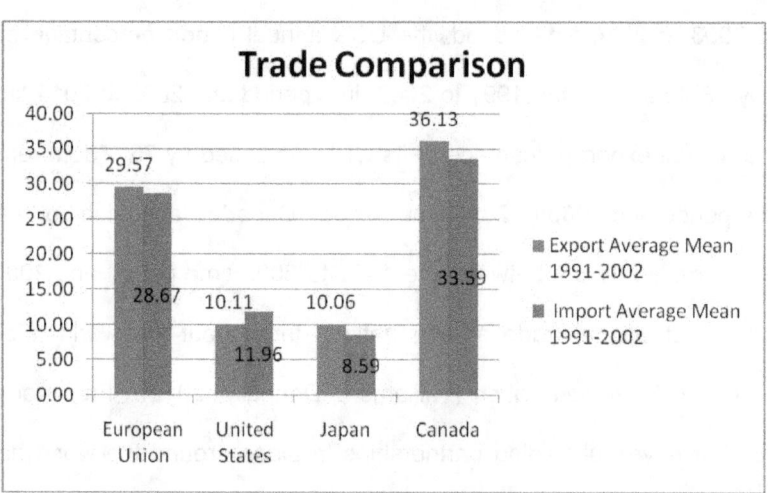

The data shows that most of the Quad nations and union had a trade surplus in an anaylsis of their annual import and export percentages of the GDP for the 1991 to 2002 time period with the exception of the US. The US showed a trade deficit of 1.85 for the 1991 to 2002 time period. The EU showed a trade surplus of .9 for the 1991 to 2002 time period, Japan showed a trade surplus of 1.47 for the 1991 to 2002 time period, and the Canada showed a trade surplus of 2.54 for the 1991 to 2002 time period. The main imports to these nations differ in relation to their economies, and their dependence on international trade for national domestic markets. The EU's main imports are machinery and vehicles, manufactured goods, energy products, chemicals, foods and drinks, and raw materials (Eurostat, 2016). The US's main imports are machines, mineral products, transportation goods, chemical products, metals, textiles, and instrumentation (Macro Connections, 2016). Japan's main imports are mineral products, machines, chemical products, textiles, metals, transportation goods, instruments, animal products, and foodstuffs. Canada's main imports are machines, transportation, mineral products, chemical products, metals, plastics and rubber, foodstuffs, textiles, and precious metals.

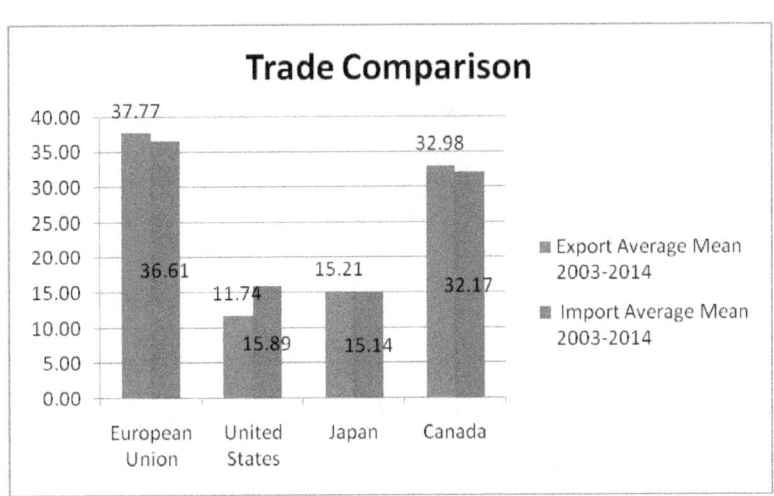

For the 2003 to 2014 time period, all of the Quad nations and union had trade surpluses with the exception of the US, which had a trade deficit of 4.15. Both imports and exports increased for most of the Quad nations and union between the two time periods measured, but Canada showed a decrease in both imports and exports between the two time periods analyzed. Although outsourcing initially increases profits for organizations, it causes sectors to become less innovative and stagnant (Stanko & Olleros, 2013). Outsourcing has shown to lead to a commoditization of ideas within industries although it increases performance and profitability in high growth industries. In situations in which outsourcing accompanies use clustering, outsourcing can benefit innovativeness, but it has a negative impact on profits. Therefore, in situations in which outsourcing leads to higher profits, it causes sectors to become less innovative, and, in situations in which clustering is used, it has a negative effect on profits, which offsets the purpose and cost savings benefit offered by outsourcing.

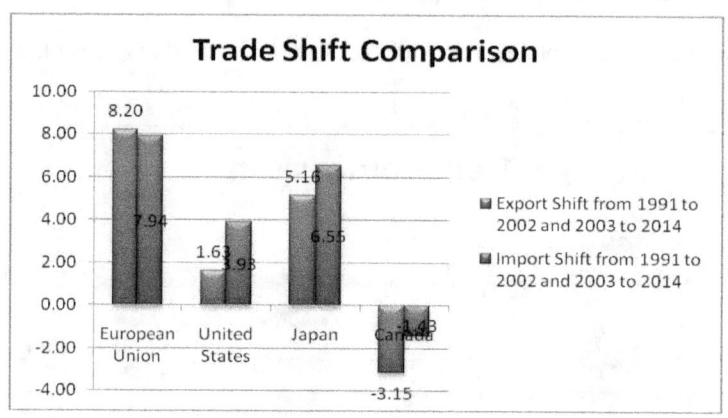

Both imports and exports of goods and services increased for all of the Quad nations and union with the exception of Canada between the two time periods measured. Canada had the highest annual import percentage of its GDP at 33.59 of all Quad nations and union during the 1991 to 2002 time period, and Canada had the highest annual export percentage of its GDP at 36.13 of all Quad nations and union during the 1991 to 2002 time period. During the 2003 to 2014 time period, Canada had the second-highest annual import percentage of its GDP at 33.59 of all Quad nations and union, and Canada had the second highest annual export percentage of its GDP at

32.98 of all Quad nations and union. The EU showed the largest annual import positive percentage shift of its GDP at 7.94 between the 1991 to 2002 and 2003 to 2014 time period of all Quad nations and union, and the EU showed the largest annual positive export percentage shift of its GDP at 8.20 between the 1991 to 2002 and 2003 to 2014 time period of all Quad nations and union. China stands out among the BRIC nations as a place to outsource to because of its highly skilled and localized workforce, which has resulted from the development of government-funded industrialized work zones (Sherlock, 2012). For developed nations' multinational corporations, the cost savings from the labor force and work zones promoted by the Chinese Government make dealing with the complex regulatory functions and corruption at the microeconomic level more bearable. Many of the BRIC nations also have highly educated people within their nations, which make them suitable locations for more complex outsourcing like research and development. Presently, nearly all the major pharmaceutical companies in the world have outsourced to China, and there are over 250 companies today in the nation focused on areas of biotech research, which has made them attractive to companies in developed nations looking to outsource for cost savings and to establish themselves for domestic market consumption through cooperating with local firms. The appeal for companies to outsource to China is the labor force's commitment to quality, performance, and service in conjunction with trainability with low staff turnover rates.

Conclusion

This study clearly shows that the annual GDP mean performance of all of the BRIC nations with the exception of the Russian Federation have increased in comparison to the 1991 to 2002 time period and the 2003 and 2014 time period. The BRIC nations had an annual GDP mean performance average percentage of change between the two periods measured of 59%. It also shows that the annual GDP performance mean of the Quad nations and union decreased significantly between the two periods measured. They had a decrease in annual GDP mean performance average percentage of change between the two periods measured of 82%. The average annual GNI mean performance for the BRIC nations between the 1991 to 2002 time period and the 2003 to 2014 time period showed a positive percentage of change of 308%. The average annual GNI mean performance for the Quad nations and union between the 1991 to 2002 time period and the 2003 to 2014 time period showed a positive percentage of change of 68%. The average annual export percentage change of the GDP of the BRIC nations between the 1991 to 2002 time period and the 2003 to 2014 time period showed a 25% increase overall for the group. The average annual export percentage change of the GDP of the Quad nations and union between the 1991 to 2002 time period and the 2003 to 2014 time period showed a 14% increase overall for the group. The average annual import percentage change of the GDP of the BRIC nations between the 1991 to 2002 time period and the 2003 to 2014 time period showed a 30% increase overall for the group. The average annual import percentage change of the GDP of the Quad nations and union between the 1991 to 2002 time period and the 2003 to 2014 time period showed a 21% increase overall for the group.

In an analysis of the annual GDP mean performance and average annual GNI mean performance of the Quad nations and union in comparison to the BRIC nations, it is clear that the BRIC nations significantly outperformed the Quad nations and union between the two time periods measured. The hypothesis that the economic performance of the BRIC nations has negatively impacted the economic growth of the Quad nations and union between the 1991 to 2002 time period and the 2003 to 2014 time period cannot conclusively be found to be true because the Quad nations and union showed good performance as a group on all measurements with the exception of the annual GDP performance mean. The annual GDP performance mean is an important indicator, and it shows that there are some systemic economic problems in the Quad nations and union related to trade deficits and imbalances. It is not clear from this analysis if the economic problems can be solely attributed to competition from the BRIC nations, but it is likely in consideration of the retail trade deficit the US has had since 1976 in conjunction with the high tariffs that are imposed by the BRIC nations on imports from other nations, specifically the Quad nations and union. In many ways, trading with the BRIC nations is not free trade, especially when considered from a developed nations' perspective in which many products from the BRIC nations and other emerging economies are able to enter the Quad nations and union duty free. The tariffs imposed by the BRIC nations on imported products from other nations have made their domestic economies less competitive and innovative, and they have effectively prohibited the consumption of non-native goods at the local level because of high prices imposed on consumers following government forced taxes. This is quite alarming coupled with the fact that developed nations, which are democratic, essentially support communistic countries, dictatorships, religious caste systems, and corrupt representative democracies by purchasing goods from BRIC nations and other emerging markets throughout the world. BRIC nations clearly have the right to govern their nations as they see fit and to impose duties on products that are imported and exported from their nations. The Quad nations and union also have the right to not trade with these nations if they feel that the ideological differences and lack of liberalization of bilateral trade between nations in the form of one-sided tariffs threatens their economic power and freedom.

Reference Citations

Alexeev, M. (2014). A Comparative Analysis of the Development of Russia, the United
      States, Europe, and China: An Interview with Michael Alexeev, *Problems of
      Economic Transition,* 56(12), p. 19-25.

Castro, T. (2013). Trade Among BRICS Countries: Changes Toward Closer
      Cooperation?, *Central European Review of Economic Issues*, 16(1), p. 131-147.

Crino, R. & Epifani, P. (2014). Trade Imbalances, Export Structure, and Wage
      Inequality, Royal Economic Society, 124(5), p. 507-540.

Daly, M. & Kuwahara, H. (1998). The Impact of the Uruguay Round on Tariff and non-
      Tariff Trade Barriers in the Quad, Blackwell Publishers, p. 207-235.

European Commision (2016). Trade: Free trade is a source of economic growth.
      Retrieved online from: http://europa.eu/pol/pdf/flipbook/en/trade_en.pdf.

Eurostat (2016). Extra-EU trade in goods. Retrieved online from:
      http://ec.europa.eu/eurostat/statistics-explained/index.php/Extra-
      EU_trade_in_goods.

Eurostat (2016). International trade in goods. Retrieved online from:
      http://ec.europa.eu/eurostat/statistics-
      explained/index.php/International_trade_in_goods#Analysis_of_main_product_gr
      oups.

Investopedia (2016). Balance of Trade. Retrieved online from:
      http://www.investopedia.com/terms/b/bot.asp?layout=infini&v=5C&adtest=5C&at
      o=3000.

Investopedia (2016). Breaking Down the Balance of Trade. Retrieved online from:
      http://www.investopedia.com/articles/forex/082913/breaking-down-balance-
      trade.asp?o=40186&l=dir&qsrc=999&qo=investopediaSiteSearch.

Investopedia (2016). Exports. Retrieved online from:
      http://www.investopedia.com/terms/e/export.asp?o=40186&l=dir&qsrc=1&qo=ser
      pSearchTopBox&ap=investopedia.com&layout=infini&v=5C&orig=1&adtest=5C.

Investopedia (2016). Gross National Income. Retrieved online from:
      http://www.investopedia.com/terms/g/gross-national-income-
      gni.asp?o=40186&l=dir&qsrc=999&qo=investopediaSiteSearch&layout=infini&v=
      5C&orig=1&adtest=5C.

Investopedia (2016). Imports. Retrieved online from:
    http://www.investopedia.com/terms/i/import.asp?layout=infini&v=5C&adtest=5C&ato=3000.

Investopedia (2016). What is GDP and why is it so important to economists and
    investors? Retrieve online from:
    http://www.investopedia.com/ask/answers/199.asp.

Kapas, M. & Liang, Y. (2009). Sizing up the Middle Class in Developing Countries,
    Journal of Portfolio Management, 35(5), p. 133-140.

Koumparoulis, D. (2014). BRICs versus other Emerging Economies: The case of India,
    International Journal of Advanced Multidisciplinary Research and Review, 2(3),
    p. 115-121.

Kumar, S. (2013). Offshoring and Trade Balance in Developed and Emerging
    Economies, *Review of Development Economics*, 18(2), p. 342-351.

Macro Connections (2016). The Observatory of Economic Complexity. Retrieved
    online from: http://macroconnections.media.mit.edu/

Mandel, B. (2012). Why is the US Share of World Merchandise Shrinking?, Federal
    Reserve Bank in New York: Economics and Finance, 18(1), p. 1-11.

Maverick, JB (2015). Is gross national income or gross domestic product a better
    measure of the economic condition of a country with substantial foreign
    investment? Retrieve online from:
    http://www.investopedia.com/ask/answers/062315/gross-national-income-gni-or-gross-domestic-product-gdp-better-measure-economic-condition-country.asp?o=40186&l=dir&qsrc=999&qo=investopediaSiteSearch&ap=investopedia.com.

Sherlock, A. (2012). Outsourcing: China Take Center Stage, Applied Clinical Trials.
    Retrieved online from: http://www.appliedclinicaltrialsonline.com/.

Srinivasan, P. (2014). Causal Nexus between Export and Growth: BRICS Nations,
    Journal of Indian Management, 1(1), p. 67-80.

Stanko, M. & Olleros, X. (2013). Industry growth and the knowledge spillover regime:
    Does outsourcing harm innovativeness but help profit?, *Journal of Business
    Research*, 66(1), p. 2007-2015.

The World Bank Group (2016). Data. Retrieved online from: http://data.worldbank.org/.

The World Bank Group (2016). GNI, Atlas method. Retrieved online from: http://data.worldbank.org/indicator/NY.GNP.ATLS.CD.

Trading Economics (2016). China Balance of Trade. Retrieved online from: http://www.tradingeconomics.com/china/balance-of-trade.

Trading Economics (2016). Germany Balance of Trade. Retrieved online from: http://www.tradingeconomics.com/germany/balance-of-trade.

Willliams, B. & Donnelly, J. (2012) US International Trade: Trends and Forecasts. Retrieved online from: https://fas.org/sgp/crs/misc/RL33577.pdf.